NDA

LILY LADY

www.farwestpress.com

First Edition

ISBN 979-8-9887354-3-4

Printed in the United States of America

Cover Artwork by Gil De Ray

NON-DISCLOSURE AGREEMENT

THIS AGREEMENT (the **"Agreement"**) is entered into on this ____day of _____ between _____ (the **"Disclosing Party"**) and _____ (henceforth referred to as the "**Receiving Party"** .

The Receiving Party hereto desires to participate in_____ (the **"Transaction"**). During this time, the Disclosing Party may divulge proprietary information with the Receiving Party. In consideration of the mutual covenants in this Agreement, the receipt of which is hereby acknowledged, the above mentioned parties hereto agree as follows:

Definition of Confidential Information.

(a) For purposes of this Agreement, **"Confidential Information"** means any information that is proprietary to the Disclosing Party and not generally known to the public, however disclosed, including, but not limited to: (i) any physically identifying marks (ii) proclivities in behavior either usual or unusual in the context of the transaction (iii) any financial information or exchange of goods from or related to the Disclosing Party (iv) any specifics related to the work of the Disclosing Party (v) any information that would reasonably be recognized as confidential information of the Disclosing Party; and (vi) any information generated by the Receiving Party or formulated after the fact of the Transaction that details or reflects the events of the Transaction. All the above includes and encompasses Confidential

Information as understood by both parties.

Terms

This Agreement shall remain in effect in perpetuity. Both parties acknowledge that the Confidential Information to be disclosed hereunder is of a unique and valuable character, and the damages to the Disclosing Party that would result from the unauthorized dissemination of the Confidential Information would be impossible to calculate. Therefore, both parties hereby agree that the Disclosing Party shall be entitled to injunctive relief preventing the dissemination of any Confidential Information in violation of the terms hereof. Such injunctive relief shall be in addition to any other remedies available hereunder, whether at law or in equity. In the event of litigation relating to this Agreement, the prevailing party shall be entitled to recover its reasonable attorney's fees and expenses.

(a) This Agreement constitutes the entire understanding between the parties and supersedes any and all prior or contemporaneous understandings and agreements, whether oral or written, between the parties, with respect to the subject matter hereof. This Agreement can only be modified by a written amendment signed by the party against whom enforcement of such modification is sought.

(b) The validity, construction and performance of this Agreement shall be governed and construed in accordance with the laws of California, applicable to contracts made and to be wholly performed within such state The Federal and state courts located in California shall have sole and exclusive jurisdiction over any disputes arising under, or in any way connected with or related to, the terms of this Agreement and Receiving Party: (i) consents to personal jurisdiction therein; and (ii) waives the right to raise *forum non conveniens* or any similar objection.

(c) This Agreement is personal in nature, and neither party may directly or indirectly assign or transfer it by operation of law or otherwise without the prior written consent of the other party, whose consent will not be unreasonably withheld. All obligations contained in this Agreement shall extend to and be binding upon the parties to this Agreement and their respective successors, assigns and designees.

IN WITNESS WHEREOF, the parties hereto have executed this Agreement as of the date first above written.

Disclosing Party   **Receiving Party**

Name: ██████   Name: Lily Lady

in the jelly shoes in the romper
in the 1950s cobalt lingerie in the rainbow mesh
wrap dress
in the via 57 west in the garbutt house in the super8
off the highway in the holiday inn
in the french tips in the lavender
lotion in the megaslicks lip balm in the silver hoops
in the edition hotel in the refinery hotel
in the baccarat hotel in the dominick hotel
in the online ad in the whatsapp chat in the telegram
group in the burner thread
in the warwick hotel in ivan's castle in the soho house
in the beverly hills hotel in the marriott
in the zone in the zone in the zone in the zone in the
zone in the zone in the zone in the zone

those who came before me

vincent gallo peter thiel dov charney james franco
elon musk
goldman sachs merrill lynch charles schwab
jp morgan
blackstone skybridge millennium citadel
           blah blah blah blah blah blah blah

I LEFT LA AND YOU SPIRALED

Hey Lily,

I hope your flight back was smooth. I had lots of fun
with you on this trip, and the footage looks good.
Just wanted to check in about something. I know
I introduced you to ██████ ██████, ████ etc. as
maybe a future collaborator so I don't want to blur
the lines with them cos they're all key creative r'ships
and a lot of work has gone into building them up
for me. I don't want it to get messy and then for it
to reflect back on me. Ppl are simple and basic. So if
you can try to steer away from non-creative contact
(ie sexy stuff) with the folks I introduce you to that
would be great incl ████. No flights, no money, no
arrangements.
I'm happy to build our r'ship as I think we're cut
from the same material but if I intro you to much
more powerful ppl than ████, and ██████ later
(which I can do in time as I believe in you as an
artist!), I would def be saying this. And I'm sure I'll
believe even more once I see your film, sam's world,
@ the ace hotel screening.
I hope you don't mind me saying this. I can also
promise that I won't try anything non creative on the
folks you have introduced me to haha! I just think
keeping a pro and non-pro line helps. We can banter
or whatever, it's fun but let's keep it artistic. And if
you disagree, well just tell me to buzz off and we'll go
our own ways. I'm cool with that too :) whatever you
like, my dear.

THAT DIRECTOR YOU LIKE IS SWEATING UNDER THE COLLAR OF HIS DENIM JACKET W/ THE FUZZY LINING

Dear Lily,

Sorry about my last email. I think what happened was that I mentioned ████ the first night we met, when we were strangers and I didn't care and as we spent more time hanging, you got under my skin and typically, I started to let my deep-seated toxic masculinity take over. And I got possessive of you, my friend, my pseudo sister, my starlet. I'd never been in such a situation.

My wife said I'm a complete idiot! Anyway, see you on your next trip out here.

3:39am SMS FROM THE DIRECTOR W/ TOO MUCH TIME ON HIS HANDS

idk what to say lily...truly.
even the whole, "*well it sounds like u might be in LA, I'll prob be there in feb maybe earlier and have a million ppl i want to see...*" thing u pulled on the phone...
of course we'll see other ppl, that's implied...i'm going back to work on projects, but thought we would coordinate to be there at the same time...
even that becomes a fkn game with u...a power play...
we have these beautiful moments
...and then you just regress and
put up unnecessary boundaries.
idk why something so basic takes on a convoluted form, this power play...
we're also on totally different wavelengths on the ▮▮▮thing and i don't see it changing.
he was my friend and i introduced you two.
it was nice between us but i think it's done.
wish you all the best in ur lovely journey of self discovery and with ▮▮▮back in LA.

stomach ache when i think about los angeles*

the heaviest shoes
knee socks folded at the ankle
baggy pants
long sleeve waffle knit
crop top black sweater
blue hoodie - hood up
bomber jacket
dirty hair x snapback x sunglasses
bubble gum flavored bubble gum
noise canceling headphones
on phone w/ mom — LAX
honey what's wrong?

*you

how to be missed

1pm wake up
10 mins jumping jacks
mariah carey hot shower
moisturize x2
check bank balance
wikihow: burn bridges
bed croissant no napkin
reconsider sobriety
voicemail delete
rinse repeat

December, New York

I am not my best self
At the Apple Store in Williamsburg
The morning J train
Smells like bacon egg & cheese
Lately I won't leave the house
For under 2k meaning I don't leave much
On the table
I crush prescription ibuprofen
Under a Lisa Frank pocket knife, generic
These press on nails
These fake diamonds
— I'll do anything to avoid pain
I don't hear anything Anjali says
At the end of therapy
New phone buzzes in my pocket
I've never been a pro
At multitasking
I shake my ass
To the DJ on TV
In the Dekalb Airbnb
Dylan says you're so good
At dancing
I feel myself
Thickening
It's the porcini dumplings
I'm stuffed with
Adultery, the keeper
Of secret biographies
Scheming & plotting
The walk home
No scarf first snow

Cheeks raw in the body electric
Walt Whitman wrote

*The armies of those I love engirth me
and I engirth them*

It's sickening

lost in translation is a bad movie (or, THAT DIRECTOR STRIKES AGAIN!)

"so let me get this straight—you thought i came all
the way to los angeles to fuck you
    then go back to my wife at the end of the week?
    i came so hard last night   thinking of you
    i miss you so much when we're not together
    i can't work i can't
do anything

wouldn't it be great if ...?   we could be friends
without all the tension...
what we're building is bigger...it could ruin everything

what do you think   the server thinks   of us?
    we're the same person
    i can't believe i met you

    the light
    was so nice
    on your face
    at the theater

it's going to start
            getting messy
            don't text
til we've talked

maybe we're not   compatible
you're so fragile & i'm
not
i have a type, you know
can you put your shirt back on?

let's take some distance   i'm projecting too much
onto you   sister starlet collaborator
it's not fair to you   and actually
              maybe a bit abusive on my part

dance for me
      i want   to do all the things with you
you want to know my fantasy?   my real fantasy?

be ready at midnight
i'm outside"

soho warehouse

hearts of palm
in a hole-y ceviche
it's raining inside
raining something
biblical
the oldest
profession
or something
borrowed
crisp sheets
checkout tomorrow

the cheap gold turns my neck green
i'm a blood blister in kitten
heels at dinner   john
in sunglasses we pick
at the same paella
the silver lake cats pretend
they haven't eaten
there's a jelly layer of slime
in the fancy feast
at venice beach i read jazz
out loud while quinn
eats figs it's overcast
colin's in the water / water choppy / bless
this mess i get up
to pee behind the pier i lock
eyes with a kid   building
a sand castle i wipe
with borrowed shirt colin
tumbles i hold
my breath / he resurfaces
at the breakup cafe
julia says *what*
are your goals i'
ve been sleeping ten hours
it's not enough
there's a wire
haired dachshund at the gallery
& THIS IS NOT ART
in framed canvas   yawn
scott says *i don't know*
what to do with you desire
is too obvious

urine drips my hand
at the clinic i twist
the plastic sample top
have you thought
about prep the nurse asks
ripley brings flowers, blue
pedialyte   at five
on my mother's lap she clips
my toenails
& i yelp
like it hurts
my goal
is butter pasta
in bed   band aid
on forearm
half blood prince
on tv

MODERN LOVE IS A RESTAURANT IN BROOKLYN

can't remember if the safe word is more or stop
/   writhing on the couch i stained last week with
ESSIE NAIL COLOR 920 S'IL VOUS PLAY:
glittering lavender pink, metallic finish
 the dog's puking & i'm downtown getting paddled /
the vet said it's the liver where   am i

stopped by the apartment to grab my night guard
              i wouldn't want
  to grind my teeth   yoyo's chunks seep
into the hardwood / i'm spinning, throwing things
      in bags / ███ sits with yoyo   watches me
stuff fishnets & face cream into a jansport
      porsche to the restaurant
restaurant to the townhouse / midnight now

      ███████ says turn around & count to ten
/ jean purrs & watches with yellow eyes / phone
buzzes texts from ███
   what am i gonna do
      about all these black & blues

PLEASE PLEASE PLEASE LET ME
GET WHAT I WANT is a song by the smiths i
never relate to....

....is this a milieu poem? modern love
has a lot of patrons tonight /
God's thick

in the air tonight / mercury
in retrograde tonight / what else
can i blame my behavior on? my mom
left a voicemail
hope you're doing well, call when you can

hey lily it was great to shoot and chat...congrats on your movie...hope you get the money in time...

wanted to call and wish you sweet dreams...went straight to voicemail

i'm trying to honor what you've wanted...even though i wish there were another way

come out to LA again soon...i'm house sitting in topanga so we'd have canyon views...

it's been 34 weeks since the last backup for this iPhone... backups happen when this iPhone is connected to power, locked, and on Wi-Fi...

yankees scoreless in the sixth but i'm getting sleepy...

hey lexie angel, it's coolboy from SA

love the footage, still gonna need at least 3 pickup days at the end of the month...

AT THE MOVIE PREMIERE I CHEW ON ICE

david cronenberg remade his own movie
worse & an hour longer
i take a call
at the roxy screening
████████'s voice on the other end
don't rush through rage
don't sign any documents
i think about wet signatures
waiting
for the credits to roll
why is everyone acting so badly?
crimes of the present
how we treat each other
never thought i'd say
talk to my lawyer
in my kanye era
by that i mean
whatever you think i mean
professional handlers
sunglasses after party
i sneak away
to squirt the tincture
on my tongue, double squeeze
the brand is *Live Better*
i want to live better
i reply all
to the email thread
subject: on delusion
(the required state of the artist)

i'm making something
out of thin air
i'm the thin air
at the top

men go jogging outside in a movie once & get nominated for everything

email advance
secured award
slurring the limo
you scoff i lift
my leg to piss
the red carpet
it sometimes rains
in LA on stage
you feign surprise
turns out
you can act
your victory lap
afterparty powder
i forward the shots
from BFA to mom
(a)live from LA

On Being (a bad person)

You fly tomorrow 8am
JFK to LAX
are you going
to take a helicopter
or UberX to the airport?
alarm set for 5
I fold into you
you fold into me
airplane mode
cardio breath
let's stop
before the finish line
New York is so complicated
not enough space, my phone's
always dying
your body
isn't mine
let's play
7 minutes in heaven
it's just a sleepover, honest
honestly why does everything
have to be so serious all the time

You're in the sky
I'm still in bed
instagram selfie
jet blue first class
coconut water, extra leg room
you deserve it
I lace my running shoes

run off the NyQuil
on the Hudson River path
old stomping grounds
Goldman Sachs
breeder dogs & nut allergies

In the shower
back at your townhouse
I make a mental note to text you
great water pressure on the third floor
or
██████████
send neither

don't know what you look like in LA
but I'm defrosting the raw venison
you left
to feed Jean
the way it makes me smell
I love
my hands
like crumpled up hundreds
I rub them on my cheeks
hope the oil fills my pores
I comb my fingers through my hair
in your SpaceX shirt
the one they gave you
on the zero gravity flight
in your woolen socks,
in the height of summer
I put the thermostat at 62
the energy bill

is higher when I'm around
you won't mind
I wait
for the delivery boy
you've ordered my favorites
the vegan yogurt, it's hard to find
peaches, sun dried tomatoes
pitted olives
last night on replay

our 7 minutes are almost up
our 7 minutes are never up
burn this

odd lots

left handhold on ludlow —   everything
        tremendous
    in my femme drag

playing the role / doing the bit

what do drugstore plastic nails say
about human nature?

trading   on derivatives
of lolita   —   what am i
if not a man's creation?

 i heart NY keychains shine
under year-round   twinkle lights

is there anything   more beautiful
    than a fake   christmas tree?

the doctor said wait six weeks

i wait three
i smell
my own blood
under white tablecloth
███ gulps chablis
& orders for me
i don't wipe down
in the hotel gym
the machine
tricks me into thinking
i'm running
through a forest
i save the cashews
from delta sky club
you know the ones
w/ the gold dust
on the comedown
on the comeback
to my bagged windows
my bk mattress pad
the sea salt irritates
my oral thrush
fever sheets
days of sleep
mystery illness
urgent care
unseen
for weeks
desert sick
i am not nourished
by the supplements
i am not comforted

by the deprivation
my body is
a no-fly zone
gold dust redux
as i vomit out
Everyone

INSIDE EVERY MAN IS
A TINY LITTLE BABY

squeeze the space between his thumb and forefinger
run your nails gently on the back of his arm,
elbow to shoulder (repeat x10)
apply pressure at his temples, top of head,
back to the temples
be an active listener
say *mmmm that sounds soooo challenging*
& *wowwww your work sounds soooo important*
run your hands across his chest, say,
i can feel your heartbeat
no, no, no
i take that back
no reminders of mortality
ok try again: run your hands across his chest, say
ooooooooh, i can tell you use the gym downstairs
straddle his chest in bed
place your hands under his neck
use your thumbs to massage his neck
in circular motions
massage his ears next
apply gentle pressure to the lobes
say, *are you getting enough sleep?*
whatever his answer, reply,
awwwww that's not enough!
turn around
shimmy down towards his calves
grab his left foot
apply medium pressure at the sole
say *ughhhhhhh i wanna make you feel soooo good*

look at the ceiling fan
but not in an obvious way
become the ceiling fan
no, no, nooooooo, what are you doing?!
you're looking directly up at the ceiling fan
way too obvious
try again
feel the presence of the ceiling fan
switch to his right foot
feel your chest lift upwards
squeeze each of his toes individually
merge your chest with the ceiling fan
good, good, good this is the hardest bit
you're doing it!
spin around in a circle
that's it, aerate that room!
now look down at yourself in the bed
be the cool breeze on your own bare shoulders
enjoy the ride!

bubbles in the air
mattress
the ludlow floor
sparkling
water & red
rocket
street noise
i smell
your face / mine
the bus home
cheek to glass
it's time
to face
the music
of the night
rings
in my ears
do not disturb
the rhythm
of the air
mattress
the rhythm
of the night
where i'm meant
to be
not where i said
i'd be
city roach
underfoot
leo
on a local bus

cobra
on a plane
the photos
uploaded tomorrow
it's already
tomorrow today
pull out
sofa w/ my name on it
please
sign the dotted line
NDA

are you here for the softball tournament?
the J zipper of her juicy sweatsuit
says it all
the power
of a letter
John 1:1
in the beginning was the Word
Logos
the power of branding, logos
the power of a John
what? i say back
it's pride month
& 'cravings fulfillment center'
is the name
of the hotel snack bar
open 24 hours
i'm getting paid
to fulfill cravings
i'm 24 hours
killing time
such a violent phrase
i never played
contact sports
in school
but there's a group of kids
here for a softball tournament
apparently
i'm in the sauna in boxers
i go from fag to femme
for dinner
he orders the lobster

it's like
shooting fish in a barrel
i stab a glazed carrot
in a bed of hazelnuts
still hungry
an hour later
in the fulfillment center
swedish fish in a box
yellow
for a cheerful feeling
red
for hunger
crisp linen & cable tv
the comfort of reruns
the comfort of a hundred
clean towels
it's like the beginning again
when there was a man
sent from God
whose name was John
who will bear witness this time?
tomorrow's maid
today's softball parents
the fulfillers & the fulfilled
scribes on stationary, all
bearing hotel logos

delta airlines it's time to check in

airport spiral
i'm like
an ingrown hair
under the surface
groomed   for a life
i don't want

nike crossbody
prayer for travelers
emergency exit row
oxygen mask principle:
you first

want everything
for a second
ears pop
no control   lord
make me
an instrument

dinner at the porsche design
   sunny isles   no blinds

heard locals call it muddy-
isles, all these new buildings

i'm inside   all these new buildings
feeling touch-sensitive   kitchen appliances

host mentions the unrivaled   charm of paris
& isn't anything but steinway   garbage?

thigh welts
from jacuzzi jets

second homes, wives   i'm tryna
live half a life and toss the rest

18 U.S. Code § 2511 - Interception and disclosure of wire, oral, or electronic communications prohibited

2 (c) It shall not be unlawful under this chapter for a person acting under color of law to intercept a wire, oral, or electronic communication, where such person is a party to the communication or one of the parties to the communication has given prior consent to such interception.

New York state permits recording telephone calls and in-person conversations with the consent of at least one of the parties. Called 'one-way consent,' this law allows an individual to record a phone call or conversation without the other person's knowledge, as long as the individual making the recording is themselves party to the conversation.

California does not.

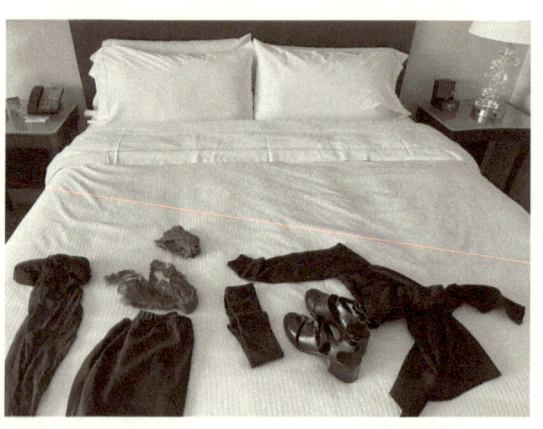

Acting class

you pull your underwear to the side
at the casa del mar hotel in santa monica
it's hard to piss in a garter belt and thigh highs

@ the penthouse

hi my name is lexie. my safe word is lemon
and i consent to being here,
voice recorder, NDA, payment.

you crawl toward the bathroom.
the wife instructs the husband to sit on the toilet.
you sit on your knees in front of him.

you think about emily, your babysitter growing
up.

call him a dirty cheating piece of shit the wife tells you.
you're a dirty cheating piece of shit you say.

she hits you on the back with a studded paddle.
say it like you mean it.

your old babysitter, emily, was about 14.

emily wanted to be an actress.
you're a dirty. cheating. piece of shit. you say.
the wife fastens a ball gag around his neck.

emily would come over on weekends.
emily had long blond hair.

you're going to fill him up, the wife says.
his eyes bulge.

she slaps him across the face.
did I say you could move?

you think about matthew mcconaughey,
how he lost 50 pounds for dallas buyers club.

you crawl to the ornate tiled sink.

you think about charlize theron,
how she let herself look so ugly in monster.

you crawl back to the couple.

you think about real life.
about aileen wuornos.
about lethal injection.

you hear the husband writhe in discomfort
you inject him with water.
you see him get hard.
you don't understand marriage.

you dip a knife into the bag of powder;
you offer each of them a hit.

what a good little slave, the wife says.

you think about your old babysitter, emily.
about the game:
you, the student. emily, the teacher.

at the casa del mar penthouse in santa monica
the wife says
take off my dress.
you unzip the black satin.

she takes the belt from his discarded pants.
she wraps the belt around your neck.
she walks you to the bedroom.
he follows on hands and knees.

you remember how emily punished you once,
during the game.
you got all the homework answers wrong, lily.

the wife holds you from behind & spreads your legs
in front of him.
is this what you wanted? she yells at him.
*is this what you were looking for when i caught you
texting the neighbor?*

no, please no, he says.
I only want you, baby.

lexie, put him in your mouth, she demands.

he hits the back of your throat.
your eyes water.
the wife has her hands on the back of your head.

you like that? she asks him.
no, i don't like it, i don't like it! he pleads, growing
harder.

you gag and cough and choke on your spit.
tears stream from your eyes.
he grabs the back of your head, too.
the wife suddenly lets go of you.

did i say you could touch her? she screams.
lexie, get me something to hit him with!

you bob back up and scan the room.
there's a book on the bedside table.
it's *the power of now* by eckhart tolle.
give it to me, now! she commands

you toss her the book and she hits him
over the head with it.
you! cheating! pig!

you think about performance...
you were never a theater kid.

get me another drink! the wife yells.
you wonder what time it is,
what you'll eat for dinner.

you slide off the bed to pour a whisky.
two of your press-on nails are broken.

bring it to me in the bathroom!
you walk into the bathroom.
she's there, peeing and checking her phone.

are you having fun? she whispers.
you nod.
okay good, me too. so much fun!
she kicks the toilet flushed and grabs the drink
from your hand.

thanks babe.
you notice the freckles on her shoulders
the band aid on her thigh.

break over
you walk back to the bedroom.
you sit on your knees in front of the husband.
you wait for your next command.

you're going to detention, emily said.
you remember believing emily.
emily was such a good actress.

the wife leaves the room again.
you stare at the husband.
you don't say anything.
you start to smile.

he breaks into a grin.
he laughs and shakes his head.
no laughing, he says, while still laughing.

the wife walks in with another bump.
lexie, rub this lube on me.
you lubricate the glittery pink dildo.

lexie, get on your back.

you think about leonardo dicaprio.
how he ate the raw liver of a bison,
& got hypothermia to prepare for the revenant.

you lie face up on the bed,
you stare at the glass chandelier.

i tried my best on the assignment, i promise!
you pleaded with emily.
you started to sob.
you ran into the bathroom and shut the door.
your six year old fingers struggled with the lock.

we're going to double penetrate you now,
the wife says.

you think about chloë sevigny.
about the unsimulated oral sex in brown bunny.

you think about how you can always tell
a movie cigarette from a real one
by the way it lights up at the tip.

you think about how emily broke character
as soon as she heard you weeping.
how she sat outside the bedroom, confused.
*it's just a game, lily. i promise
i'm not really mad at you,*

i was just pretending.

you remember how you sobbed in the bathroom.
you remember the shame.

you feel the walls of the penthouse suite cave in
& the walls of your insides expand

you breathe like tyson before a fight,
idina menzel on opening night.

the husband is on top of you.
the wife thrusts into you from below.

she reaches over you and grabs the back of his neck.
you won't get better than this baby, she says.
you just have to ask me next time.

in the elevator down to the lobby,
you wonder if paypal will ban your account again.
you check your email.

you have appeared in a recent casting search!
you thought you'd unsubscribed.

you step outside

you yell
CUT
into darkness.

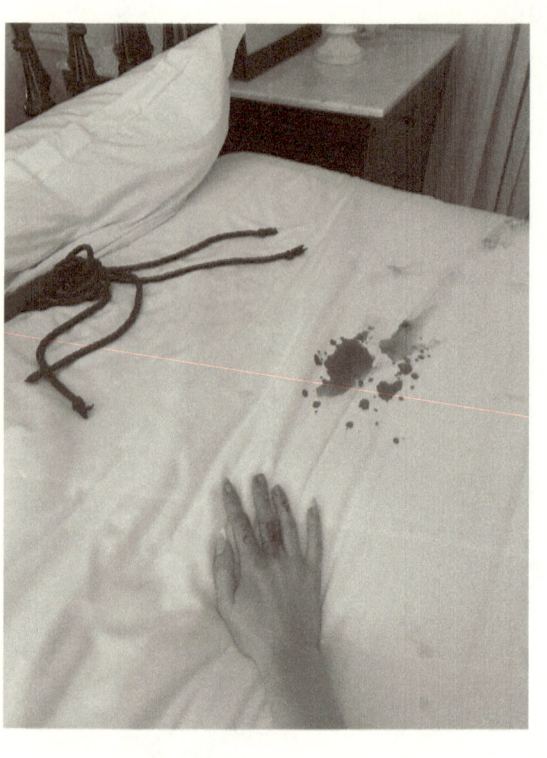

the end,
or,
some director somewhere
in silver lake feels something

Dear Lily,

Wow, your last email was so cruel! All that could've been said in a much softer and more compassionate way. Agreed, it was never a natural friendship. We are very diff ppl. It always felt laboured. Our paths just happened to cross for a few days when we needed company in LA.

Take care.

ALSO OUT ON FAR WEST

farwestpress.com

+1 (541) FAR-WEST